W9-BUI-558

Private Investigators
and
Bounty Hunters

CRIME, JUSTICE, AND PUNISHMENT

Private Investigators and Bounty Hunters

Ann G. Gaines

Austin Sarat, GENERAL EDITOR

CHELSEA HOUSE PUBLISHERS
Philadelphia

Frontis: *Scene from* The Maltese Falcon, *one of Hollywood's most popular private eye films.*

Chelsea House Publishers

Editor in Chief Stephen Reginald
Managing Editor James D. Gallagher
Production Manager Pamela Loos
Art Director Sara Davis
Director of Photography Judy L. Hasday
Senior Production Editor Lisa Chippendale

**Staff for PRIVATE INVESTIGATORS AND
          BOUNTY HUNTERS**

Senior Editor John Ziff
Contributing Editor Chandra Speeth
Associate Art Director Takeshi Takahashi
Designer Keith Trego
Picture Researcher Gillian Speeth
Cover Illustration Janet Hamlin

First Printing

1 3 5 7 9 8 6 4 2

The Chelsea House World Wide Web site address is
http://www.chelseahouse.com

Library of Congress Cataloging-in-Publication Data

Gaines, Ann G.
Private investigators and bounty hunters / Ann G. Gaines;
Austin Sarat, general editor.
p. 96 cm. — (Crime, justice, and punishment)
Includes bibliographical references and index.
Summary: Details the history and cases of private
investigators and bounty hunters and discusses their
fictional representations in novels, short stories, motion
pictures, and television shows.

ISBN 0-7910-4285-5 (hardcover)

1. Private investigators—United States—Juvenile
literature. 2. Crime—United States—Juvenile literature.
[1. Private investigators. 2. Crime.] I. Title. II. Series.
HV8088.G338 1999
363.28'9—dc21
                                    98-56198
                                    CIP

Contents

CRIME, JUSTICE, AND PUNISHMENT

Fears and Fascinations:

An Introduction to Crime, Justice, and Punishment

By Austin Sarat

We live with crime and images of crime all around us. Crime evokes in most of us a deep aversion, a feeling of profound vulnerability, but it also evokes an equally deep fascination. Today, in major American cities the fear of crime is a major fact of life, some would say a disproportionate response to the realities of crime. Yet the fear of crime is real, palpable in the quickened steps and furtive glances of people walking down darkened streets. At the same time, we eagerly follow crime stories on television and in movies. We watch with a "who done it" curiosity, eager to see the illicit deed done, the investigation undertaken, the miscreant brought to justice and given his just deserts. On the streets the presence of crime is a reminder of our own vulnerability and the precariousness of our taken-for-granted rights and freedoms. On television and in the movies the crime story gives us a chance to probe our own darker motives, to ask "Is there a criminal within?" as well as to feel the collective satisfaction of seeing justice done.

Fear and fascination, these two poles of our engagement with crime, are, of course, only part of the story. Crime is, after all, a major social and legal problem, not just an issue of our individual psychology. Politicians today use our fear of, and fascination with, crime for political advantage. How we respond to crime, as well as to the political uses of the crime issue, tells us a lot about who we are as a people as well as what we value and what we tolerate. Is our response compassionate or severe? Do we seek to understand or to punish, to enact an angry vengeance or to rehabilitate and welcome the criminal back into our midst? The CRIME, JUSTICE, AND PUNISHMENT series is designed to explore these themes, to ask why we are fearful and fascinated, to probe the meanings and motivations of crimes and criminals and of our responses to them, and, finally, to ask what we can learn about ourselves and the society in which we live by examining our responses to crime.

Crime is always a challenge to the prevailing normative order and a test of the values and commitments of law-abiding people. It is sometimes a Raskolnikov-like act of defiance, an assertion of the unwillingness of some to live according to the rules of conduct laid out by organized society. In this sense, crime marks the limits of the law and reminds us of law's all-too-regular failures. Yet sometimes there is more desperation than defiance in criminal acts; sometimes they signal a deep pathology or need in the criminal. To confront crime is thus also to come face-to-face with the reality of social difference, of class privilege and extreme deprivation, of race and racism, of children neglected, abandoned, or abused whose response is to enact on others what they have experienced themselves. And occasionally crime, or what is labeled a criminal act, represents a call for justice, an appeal to a higher moral order against the inadequacies of existing law.

Figuring out the meaning of crime and the motivations of criminals and whether crime arises from defiance, desperation, or the appeal for justice is never an easy task. The motivations and meanings of crime are as varied as are the persons who engage in criminal conduct. They are as mysterious as any of the mysteries of the human soul. Yet the desire to know the secrets of crime and the criminal is a strong one, for in that knowledge may lie one step on the road to protection, if not an assurance of one's own personal safety. Nonetheless, as strong as that desire may be, there is no available technology that can allow us to know the whys of crime with much confidence, let alone a scientific certainty. We can, however, capture something about crime by studying the defiance, desperation, and quest for justice that may be associated with it. Books in the CRIME, JUSTICE, AND PUNISHMENT series will take up that challenge. They tell stories of crime and criminals, some famous, most not, some glamorous and exciting, most mundane and commonplace.

This series will, in addition, take a sober look at American criminal justice, at the procedures through which we investigate crimes and identify criminals, at the institutions in which innocence or guilt is determined. In these procedures and institutions we confront the thrill of the chase as well as the challenge of protecting the rights of those who defy our laws. It is through the efficiency and dedication of law enforcement that we might capture the criminal; it is in the rare instances of their corruption or brutality that we feel perhaps our deepest betrayal. Police, prosecutors, defense lawyers, judges, and jurors administer criminal justice and in their daily actions give substance to the guarantees of the Bill of Rights. What is an adversarial system of justice? How does it work? Why do we have it? Books in the CRIME, JUSTICE, AND PUNISHMENT series will examine the thrill of the chase as we seek to capture the criminal. They will also reveal the drama and majesty of the criminal trial as well as the day-to-day reality of a criminal justice system in which trials are the exception and negotiated pleas of guilty are the rule.

When the trial is over or the plea has been entered, when we have separated the innocent from the guilty, the moment of punishment has arrived. The injunction to punish the guilty, to respond to pain inflicted by inflicting pain, is as old as civilization itself. "An eye for an eye and a tooth for a tooth" is a biblical reminder that punishment must measure pain for pain. But our response to the criminal must be better than and different from the crime itself. The biblical admonition, along with the constitutional prohibition of "cruel and unusual punishment," signals that we seek to punish justly and to be just not only in the determination of who can and should be punished, but in how we punish as well. But neither reminder tells us what to do with the wrongdoer. Do we rape the rapist, or burn the home of the arsonist? Surely justice and decency say no. But, if not, then how can and should we punish? In a world in which punishment is neither identical to the crime nor an automatic response to it, choices must be made and we must make them. Books in the CRIME, JUSTICE, AND PUNISHMENT series will examine those choices and the practices, and politics, of punishment. How do we punish and why do we punish as we do? What can we learn about the rationality and appropriateness of today's responses to crime by examining our past and its responses? What works? Is there, and can there be, a just measure of pain?

CRIME, JUSTICE, AND PUNISHMENT brings together books on some of the great themes of human social life. The books in this series capture our fear and fascination with crime and examine our responses to it. They remind us of the deadly seriousness of these subjects. They bring together themes in law, literature, and popular culture to challenge us to think again, to think anew, about subjects that go to the heart of who we are and how we can and will live together.

*   *   *   *   *

We often think of law enforcement as a purely public matter, a core governmental activity. But in the past as well as today, the job of dealing with crime and of apprehending criminals has straddled the line between public and private, between the world of police and the world of private investigators. Sometimes those worlds have complemented each other, sometimes they have not. Sometimes one would be effective and free of corruption while the other would not. How, whether, and when these parallel systems of law enforcement come together has long been a major issue facing the criminal justice system.

The importance of this issue is certainly as great now as it has ever been. More and more American citizens and businesses rely on private security, not just to apprehend criminals, but to provide a network of protection above and beyond what the police provide. Who are the people in the business of selling security? What do they do? Who are their historical antecedents? What questions does the spread of private security raise about our safety and our civil liberties?

Private Investigators and Bounty Hunters provides answers to these and other pressing questions. Interspersing lively stories of heroic and infamous figures with penetrating historical analysis, this book provides a well-balanced overview of an area that, for too long, has been ignored. It explores the many roles that private security and investigators now play and offers a glimpse of their place in the popular imagination. In the end it suggests that we need to address many complex matters if we are to live safely and comfortably in a world of private eyes and bounty hunters.

PRIVATE AGENTS IN A PUBLIC ARENA

A t 2 A.M. one warm night, Hillary Bingham woke up in her bed, thirsty. The 27-year-old woman, a successful advertising agent, lived alone in a Victorian-style apartment in Boston's Beacon Hill section. After going into the kitchen and getting a glass of juice, she returned to bed and fell sound asleep.

Some time later, she awoke with a knife at her throat. A thin man with jet-black hair and a long scar running across his forehead and down to the bridge of his nose told her not to scream or he would kill her. When Bingham tried to move, the man pressed the knife closer to her throat. Then he slipped into the bed and raped her. After the assault, the man made Bingham drink a cup of coffee with him at the kitchen table. He then forced her back into the bedroom and

Private investigators and bounty hunters occupy unique niches at the margins of American law enforcement.

raped her again. This cycle continued until seven o'clock, when the assailant left, taking Bingham's money and her address book. "Maybe we can do this again sometime," he said ominously.

After wandering aimlessly for hours through the streets of Boston, Bingham recovered from her shock, went to a police station, and reported the rape. She gave police a detailed description of the rapist and, in response to the officers' questions, described her ordeal minutely. Based on the rapist's parting words and on the fact that he had taken her address book, the lieutenant on duty believed the rapist might try to contact Bingham again, and this could provide an opportunity to catch him.

In the middle of the following week, Bingham received a call at work from the rapist. Following the police officers' instructions, she told the man that she had enjoyed making love to him and that she wanted to see him again. He said he would drop by her apartment on Saturday.

When Bingham notified the police lieutenant of the call, he told her he would assign a four-man team of undercover police officers to monitor her apartment on Saturday and to apprehend the rapist if he showed up. Because she was nervous about being in the apartment alone, however, Bingham asked a girlfriend of hers to stay with her.

On Saturday night at 10:30, there was a loud knock on the door of Bingham's apartment. Certain it was the police wanting to tell her they had caught her assailant, and relieved that her ordeal was over, Bingham opened the door. There, alone, stood the rapist.

Fortunately, Bingham's friend rushed to the door, and together the two women managed to shove it closed and lock it, after which they heard the rapist running away. Bingham called the police immediately. She discovered that the lieutenant who had been handling her case was off-duty, and no one at the police station

Tailing a subject in a crowd is an art form, requiring the private detective to be observant yet inconspicuous.

seemed to know about a stakeout at her apartment. Evidently there had been a breakdown in communications.

Frightened that the rapist was still on the loose, and exasperated with the police, Bingham told her story to her uncle, who suggested that they hire a private investigator. They called a man named Gil Lewis.

Just as the police had done, Lewis asked Bingham to tell him the whole story of the assault, and he, too, asked for a detailed description of the rapist. But then he began a more unconventional investigation of the incident. Lewis asked Bingham to take him to her apartment and to walk him through all the events of that night. He had Bingham act out the rapist's gestures and his way of carrying himself. Lewis observed that Bingham kept her elbows tucked in close to her body as she moved around the apartment. He felt this meant that the rapist was accustomed to negotiating a tight space. From this information he surmised that Bingham's rapist might be a "food guy," a worker in a crowded kitchen. He refused to call this theory a hunch, preferring instead to chalk it up to his 20 years of experience in the field.

Lewis initiated "protective surveillance" of Bingham: he followed her in the same way he might shadow a suspicious individual, but with the purpose of guarding her rather than gathering information. For the next few weeks, the private investigator followed his client wherever she went. He watched her out of the corners of his eyes, in reflections in mirrors. He never looks the person he's shadowing right in the eye, even when that person, like Bingham, is a client under protective surveillance. To do so might tip off a stalker.

Lewis managed to follow Bingham so unobtrusively that, after a few days under his protective surveillance, she called him in a panic. Because she hadn't seen him, she believed that he had backed out on her. It was only when Lewis told her exactly what was on the salad she had eaten that day for lunch that Bingham was convinced she was in good hands.

When Lewis wasn't shadowing Bingham, he was inquiring into the identity of her rapist. Such questioning can be a wild-goose chase, but marks like distinctive scars or tattoos are a big help in tracking down a suspect. After three weeks of questioning and searching, Lewis got lucky. He found a security chief at a local hospital who recognized the description of the man with the scar and identified him as Federico Vargas.

Vargas had been employed at the hospital's cafeteria grill, an occupation that fit exactly with Lewis's con-jecture. Unfortunately, he had quit his job just two weeks earlier. Lewis checked Vargas's public records and discovered that the assault on Hillary Bingham was not his first offense. In fact, he was wanted in Texas for raping a 15-year-old girl.

With this new information, Lewis could identify the man, could probably track him down, and could make a plausible case that the man was Bingham's assailant. But the private investigator knew that the only way to ensure a conviction would be to catch Var-gas in the act of threatening Bingham.

A few days later, Vargas called Bingham at work again. Following Lewis's instructions, she told Vargas that she was in a meeting and asked him to call her back in an hour. This provided enough time for Lewis to have the call traced to a telephone booth in Dor-chester, at the corner of 8th and Weld.

Now Lewis knew that it was time to give the infor-mation to the police so that they could make a formal arrest. Private investigators have no special law enforcement powers; they can only arrest someone in the act of committing a felony, a privilege granted to all citizens.

One hour later, Bingham's office phone rang again. The rapist was furious that she had turned him away on Saturday night. Then Bingham heard the sound of a scuffle at the other end of the line. The next voice on the phone was that of a Boston police officer who informed her that her assailant had just been arrested.

Making an arrest was the reason Hector Rivera traveled to Seaside, a small city south of Santa Cruz along the California coast. Like private eye Gil Lewis, Rivera was acting on behalf of a paying client. Unlike Lewis, he brought broad law enforcement powers to his task, including the power to arrest people not engaged in the commission of a felony.

The man Rivera was looking for in Seaside lived in a housing project. Rivera located the address and observed the entrance for a while. Noticing nothing out of the ordinary, he approached the door and, without knocking or otherwise announcing his presence, kicked it down.

Inside, he found a startled family in the middle of dinner. Rivera spotted his man and bounded toward him, handcuffs at the ready. But the man resisted, and upon hearing the loud struggle that ensued, neighbors rushed in through the broken door. As they surrounded him, Rivera announced that he was a bounty hunter and that the man he was trying to arrest had skipped bail—that is, had failed to appear for his criminal trial, leaving the bail bondsman Rivera was working for financially liable. But the neighbors angrily insisted that he leave, and as they hissed threats and Rivera snarled counterthreats, the fugitive bolted out the back door.

Rivera broke free of the small mob and gave chase. Across the backyards of neighbors, over fences, he pursued the fugitive, finally dragging him down and handcuffing him. When he hauled the fugitive to his car, the man's family and neighbors were waiting. Although they screamed at Rivera, no one made any move to physically stop him. Rivera loaded the suspect into his car and drove off, having earned another paycheck of about $1,000.

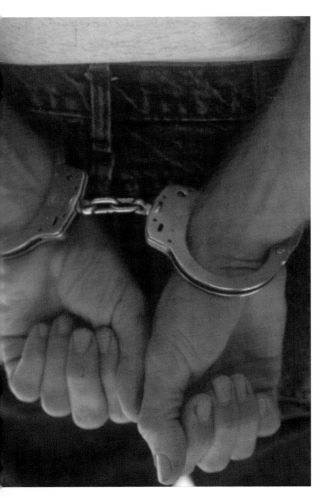

Bounty hunters arrest thousands of fugitives every year.

We usually think of law enforcement as an official, public function: local police departments, supplemented perhaps by state police or federal organizations such as the Federal Bureau of Investigation (FBI), detect, investigate, and solve crimes and apprehend criminals. But the law enforcement arena also contains tens of thousands of unofficial or quasi-official actors (in this context meaning anyone who has a professional function), of whom private eye Gil Lewis and bounty hunter Hector Rivera are two examples.

Private investigators and bounty hunters play important and multifaceted—if often misunderstood— roles. In some ways these private actors highlight the weaknesses and limitations of official law enforcement; in some ways they complement the police; in some ways they constitute a type of freelance police force independent of the authorities. Sometimes their functions overlap police responsibilities; sometimes they specialize in tasks the police aren't particularly good at or simply aren't responsible for.

In their dealings with both crime suspects and ordinary citizens, private investigators (who are variously also called "private detectives" and "private eyes") have considerably less power than the police. In many ways bounty hunters actually have more, for they aren't constrained by constitutional and procedural safeguards of suspects' rights.

The prominence of private agents in American law enforcement is somewhat anomalous. This curious situation has its origins in a time when law enforcement was completely different from what it is today, a time when organized, official police units were in their infancy and when much of the country lacked significant police protection.

THE BIRTH OF PRIVATE DETECTIVES

Urban growth, fed in large part by immigration, fueled big increases in crime in the 19th century, which in turn led to the establishment of permanent police forces and to the rise of private police agencies. Pictured here: "Tenement Alley," one of New York City's toughest sections, circa 1890.

Throughout the colonial period, the task of policing American communities fell largely upon private citizens. As in England, American colonial villages had constables, officials whose primary function was to keep the peace and who frequently were on duty only at night. In the countryside, sheriffs performed some law enforcement duties over a fairly large area but were primarily responsible for executing the orders of judges and courts. Even in more urban areas there was relatively little criminal activity, and crime detection and prevention largely boiled down to vigilance on the part of the members of a community, who were expected to look out for one another. In some communities, male citizens took turns on "night watch," during which several men patrolled the village looking for signs of criminal activity or for fires. If they found anything suspicious, they would call out, alerting everyone to the emergency and summoning other citizens to their aid. During the day, crime wasn't

A night watchman in New Amsterdam (New York City) takes some refreshment at the end of his shift. Throughout the colonial period, American communities made do without daytime police protection.

a major concern, and organized police departments weren't needed or wanted.

For the most part, this situation prevailed for the first few decades after independence. But when immigration spurred the growth of cities, crime there increased enormously. Constables and sheriffs proved insufficient for the increasingly difficult task of preventing, detecting, and investigating crime. By midcentury the larger American cities had created permanent, professional police departments. Outside city limits, however, law enforcement remained minimal.

The creation of urban police departments did not mean an end to city dwellers' crime problems. The police were often viewed as inept and corrupt, a perception that would remain—in most cases, justifiably—until the end of the 19th century. Indeed, early American police departments were typically under the control of the city's mayor, and policemen were often appointed solely on the basis of their loyalty to him. Worse, police forces were frequently used as a tool to intimidate and punish the mayor's political opponents, who might find themselves harassed by the police or with no police protection when they most needed it.

The case of Chicago mayor Levi D. Boone is illustrative. In 1855 Boone was elected on the Know-Nothing ticket (the Know-Nothings were an anti-Catholic, anti-immigrant party). He quickly dismissed Chicago's constable force, which was largely foreign-born, and replaced it with a uniformed police force consisting of 80 hand-picked supporters. Although Boone initiated welcome reforms, establishing a three-shift-a-day routine for his officers and setting them on regular patrols of the city's neighborhoods, police protection was available only for his political allies. When Stephen Douglas, a prominent Illinois politician and future presidential candidate, spoke in Chicago against the Know-Nothing Party, Boone's police made no attempt to stop a crowd of Know-Nothing supporters from mobbing him. As a result of that incident and others like it, ordinary citizens lost faith in the police force's willingness and ability to protect them.

In this climate of fear and distrust, private police companies emerged to fill the void. In March 1857, Cyrus Bradley, the former chief of police under Mayor Boone, established the Chicago Detecting and Collecting Police Agency, which offered police services for a fee. Bradley's police were an immediate success. The new Chicago mayor, Republican John Wentworth, soon complained in a newspaper editorial,

[I]t is a lamentable fact that whilst our citizens are heavily taxed to support a large police force, a highly respectable private police is doing a lucrative business. Our citizens have ceased to look to the public police for protection, for the detection of culprits, or the recovery of stolen property.

In 1858 the Merchant's Police Company was formed in Chicago under the direction of G. T. Moore. He charged his customers, the city's businesses, 50 cents a week for protection. Describing his policy to potential customers, Moore declared, "We take small beats, so that we are able to visit the alleys and streets four or five times an hour, and once each hour we try each subscriber's door."

Even as city police departments began to grow, the private police market boomed, for the regular police had little incentive to be either efficient or honest, leaving many citizens dissatisfied. Private companies competed not so much with the public police but with one another, and their best customers were businesses.

Although a number of private police agencies flourished, one organization came to dominate the market. Its name became virtually synonymous with "private eye," and its founder, a Scottish immigrant and erstwhile barrel maker, forged a reputation as one of the world's greatest detectives—a reputation that survives to this day.

Allan Pinkerton got into the private detective business somewhat by accident. After emigrating from Scotland with his wife, he settled in Dundee, an Illinois town northwest of Chicago on the Fox River, where he established a successful barrel-making operation. One day, while surveying an uninhabited island in the river for trees from which to make barrels, Pinkerton stumbled upon the camp of a group of counterfeiters. He reported his discovery to the local sheriff, whom he later assisted in apprehending the counterfeiters. His appetite for investigation whetted, Pinkerton became deputy sheriff

The policemen of New York City's 20th Precinct, 1880s. Corruption and incompetence among the regular police paved the way for private police services.

of Cook County and eventually abandoned barrelmaking to set up his own detective agency in partnership with a local attorney, Edward A. Rucker, in 1850. The men called their firm the North-Western Police Agency. By 1852 North-Western had become the now-famous Pinkerton National Detective Agency.

Business boomed, and Pinkerton shrewdly recognized that there was money to be made outside the confines of cities and towns. On February 1, 1855, he signed a contract to protect six railroads for a yearly retainer of $10,000.

Legendary private detective Allan Pinkerton earned a reputation for cleverness, tenacity, and honesty.

In 1858 Pinkerton established Pinkerton's Protective Police Patrol, a small group of uniformed patrolmen, to guard local businesses. In its first year of operation, it reported 751 cases of unlocked doors or windows and 440 cases of improper employee conduct. Pinkerton's police soon received the power to make arrests, which they exercised 53 times that year. The Chicago Police Department also hired Pinkerton's police, at a cost of $700, to watch for pickpockets during the holiday season.

Although providing police protection and security

services to clients would become a substantial part of Pinkerton's business, it was the daring exploits of the Pinkerton detectives that captured the imagination of the country. In many respects these were America's original private eyes. Like their leader, the Pinkerton detectives earned a reputation for doggedness, skill, and cunning in pursuing those who had committed crimes against Pinkerton clients.

They also earned a reputation for integrity. In large measure this was the result of the strict code of ethics Allan Pinkerton established for his company and its employees. His firm would not take part in divorce cases or cases involving official corruption. His detectives would receive no tips or rewards for their services, nor would they coerce testimony through drugs or liquor.

Pinkerton also seemed to be an extraordinary judge of character. He claimed that to be employed by his agency, a man really needed only three things: honesty, morality, and common sense. Indeed, a Pinkerton agent didn't even necessarily need to be a man: a woman named Kate Warne became Pinkerton's first female operative and the first female detective in the United States. Pinkerton seldom hired former constables, instead drawing his operatives from all walks of life and training them in his own methods of surveillance, tracking, and detection. Pinkerton placed great emphasis on undercover techniques, and his detectives became masters of disguise and role playing. The boss himself had a large closet in his Chicago office filled with various disguises, which he used in the cases he personally investigated.

Disguise would play a vital role in what was perhaps Pinkerton's most famous case, one that involved rumors of a plot to assassinate Abraham Lincoln before he assumed the presidency. In 1861 Pinkerton was hired to protect Lincoln during the president-elect's journey from his hometown of Springfield, Illinois, to Washington, D.C. The train trip would take Lincoln east to

Pennsylvania and then south through Maryland to the nation's capital. Along the way he would make many stops to deliver speeches.

Lincoln boarded his train without incident. Meanwhile, Pinkerton and one of his agents went to Baltimore to assess the situation in that stronghold of anti-Lincoln, proslavery sentiment. There the detectives picked up hints of a plot to assassinate Lincoln after he changed trains in Baltimore. Pinkerton immediately headed for Pennsylvania to warn the president-elect, but Lincoln refused to change his plans based on rumor alone. He was determined to continue on to Washington as intended. However, when a second warning came via a sealed letter from his own political supporters, Lincoln became convinced that the threat was real, and he allowed Pinkerton to take over.

In Harrisburg—according to one version of events —the detective disguised Lincoln as an old lady, complete with a shawl about his shoulders and an old, soft hat on his head. He moved the president-elect onto a different train, which headed for Washington without stopping. Pinkerton placed special agents along the route and cut all the telegraph wires so that no word of the switch could reach any would-be assassins. Lincoln passed through Baltimore without incident and arrived safely in Washington for his inauguration. Whether the rumored assassination plot was genuine has never been confirmed.

In the years following the Civil War's end in 1865, Americans began looking westward again. Homesteaders flocked to the prairie to plow under the sod for farmland, cattlemen established sprawling ranches, and frontier towns sprang up like weeds after a rainfall. By the end of the 1860s, a transcontinental railroad linking the East Coast with the West had been completed, and thousands of miles of new track had been laid, greatly facilitating the movement of people and goods. For all the activity, however, the West remained sparsely populated, a vast, empty ocean surrounding tiny islands of human settlement.

Law enforcement reflected this situation. Within the confines of a town, the sheriff maintained order; at the edge of town, the level of law enforcement fell off significantly. For example, a San Francisco–to–Chicago train would be protected before it left the Bay Area and after it arrived in the Windy City, but in between lay miles and miles of open terrain.

These large gaps in law enforcement tempted outlaws. Bank robbers realized that if they got out of town unscathed, there was a good chance they could elude the sheriff's posse. Trains were potentially even better targets than banks. Many carried thousands of dollars in cash, and wealthy passengers could also be robbed. But most important, outlaws could choose the best place along the line to strike and could then effect a quick escape before law enforcement had a chance to join the chase. There existed no national law enforcement agency like today's FBI to pursue outlaws across jurisdictions.

In effect, however, the Pinkertons functioned as a private version of such an agency. When a bank, express service, or train protected by the Pinkerton National Detective Agency was robbed, Pinkerton detectives pursued the case to its conclusion, regardless of the time, expense, or distance involved. The company's logo, consisting of the words "We never sleep" printed around the image of an unblinking eye, symbolized for thieves and the law-abiding alike an ever-vigilant crime-fighting force. (Allan Pinkerton himself was dubbed "the Eye." Contrary to popular belief, however, this is not where the term *private eye* originated; the "eye" actually arose as a phonetic substitution for the letter *i*, an abbreviation of "investigator.")

For the Pinkerton agency, the period between the end of the Civil War and the turn of the century was a fabled era, as the criminals the company pursued

President-elect Abraham Lincoln en route to Washington, D.C. Allan Pinkerton may have foiled an assassination attempt during this journey by disguising Lincoln as an old woman.

formed a veritable who's who of the Wild West's legendary bank and train robbers, including Jesse and Frank James; the Younger brothers; and Butch Cassidy, the Sundance Kid, and the rest of the Wild Bunch. This was also arguably the most important era in the history of private detectives in America, for in certain areas of the country the Pinkertons (and, to a lesser extent, the other private detective agencies that arose to compete with them) were virtually the only law.

The first train robbery in the United States is attributed to the Reno Gang, a notorious group of outlaws headquartered in the southern Indiana town of Seymour. On October 6, 1866, brothers John and Simeon Reno, along with another gang member named Franklin Sparks, boarded an Ohio & Mississippi Railroad train in Seymour. As soon as the train left the station, they knocked out the guard for the Adams Express Company, which was transporting $45,000 in cash and gold in two safes on the train. A few miles down the track, where other members of the gang were waiting with horses, the bandits pushed the safes off the train. Though they couldn't break open the larger of the two safes, they did get $15,000—a considerable sum in those days—from the smaller one before riding off. The Adams Express Company quickly contacted Allan Pinkerton.

Pinkerton soon knew who was responsible for the robbery. But bringing them to justice would be no simple matter. Trying to capture the Reno Gang through a direct assault on their stronghold in Seymour would endanger scores of innocent citizens. And because the local community had, over the years, been thoroughly terrorized by the outlaws, their cooperation was unlikely. Nor was it likely that a jury anywhere in southern Indiana would convict the Renos.

Pinkerton conceived a plan to throw the gang into disarray by kidnapping its leader, John Reno. He sent several Pinkerton agents undercover into Seymour to lay the groundwork. One got a job at the railroad depot. Another posed as a gambler and soon established his headquarters at the Renos' favorite saloon. Pinkerton even managed to recruit the owner of that saloon, Dick Winscott, for his plan. Months passed as the Pinkerton detectives blended into the community and gained the trust of the gang.

In the meantime, the Renos continued their criminal activities, stealing $22,000 from the Daviess County Treasury in Gallatin, Missouri. Learning of that heist, Allan Pinkerton wired the sheriff of Gallatin, who got a writ for John Reno's arrest and joined Pinkerton and six of his detectives on a special train that waited on a railroad siding several miles outside Seymour. Pinkerton got word to saloon keeper Dick Winscott to find some excuse to bring John Reno to the railway depot. Winscott and Reno were on the platform waiting for the afternoon express when Pinkerton's special train slowly pulled into the station. The six Pinkerton detectives jumped to the platform, grabbed Reno, and wrestled him aboard the still-moving train. By the time the other members of the Reno Gang received word of the kidnapping, it was too late to catch Pinkerton's train.

John Reno was taken far from his home turf in Indiana to Gallatin, Missouri, where he was tried for the Daviess County robbery, convicted, and sentenced to a prison term in a Missouri penitentiary. But if Pinkerton thought this would strike a crippling blow to the Reno Gang, he was sadly mistaken. Back in Indiana, John Reno's brother Frank assumed control of the gang and led his men on a crime spree that included robberies of post offices, trains, and county treasuries.

The Pinkerton agency remained on the Reno case. In March 1868 Pinkerton detectives tracked Frank Reno and three associates to a farmhouse in Council Bluffs, Iowa. Storming the house, they surprised the outlaws, who were in the middle of breakfast. The Pinkertons arrested the four and took them to the local jail. But Allan Pinkerton soon received a telegram informing him that the men had broken out. Above the hole in the wall through which the outlaws had made their escape they had written, "April's Fool." It was April 1, 1868.

Only a month later, Frank Reno led some two dozen outlaws on his gang's most lucrative robbery. The

Train robbers like the Reno and James gangs made up some of the Pinkerton agency's most famous and dangerous adversaries.

bandits boarded an Ohio and Mississippi Valley train that was stopped at a watering station near Seymour. After beating up the engineer and fireman and shooting the conductor, they uncoupled the engine and express cars from the rest of the train and started off. They then burst through the express car door and threw the startled Adams Express Company guard off the train. Before abandoning the train and escaping on horses waiting down the line, the Reno Gang removed $96,000 in cash and bonds from two safes.

After the robbery, the gang split up. Frank Reno and three others went to Canada; Simeon and William Reno, to Minneapolis. Three other gang members rode to Coles County, Illinois, where Pinkerton detectives, in conjunction with local sheriffs, soon located and arrested them. Vigilantes lynched the three outlaws as they were being transported back to Indiana to stand trial.

On July 22 a Pinkerton detective named William Stiggart arrested William and Simeon Reno, who had returned to Indiana from Minneapolis. The outlaws landed in Indiana's New Albany Jail. Of the four out-

Above: The Kearney, Missouri, homestead of Zerelda Samuels, mother of Jesse and Frank James. When Pinkerton detectives seeking to capture the outlaw brothers tossed a bomb into the house, they succeeded only in killing the Jameses' half-brother, Archie (facing page)—and in bringing widespread condemnation upon Allan Pinkerton and his detective agency.

law Reno brothers, that left only Frank still at large.

The Pinkertons soon learned that Frank Reno and three other members of his gang were holed up in a small house in Windsor, Canada, just across the border from Detroit. Allan Pinkerton himself led a small party of detectives and local deputies to Windsor and apprehended the four men, one of whom was released for lack of evidence. After Canada extradited the three remaining gang members to the United States to stand trial, they were taken to the New Albany Jail, the same one that housed Simeon and William Reno. The outlaws never did get their day in court, however. On the night of December 12, 1868, a large group of hooded vigilantes forced their way into the jail and hanged the Reno brothers and their fellow gang members.

The Pinkertons' dogged, two-year pursuit of the Reno Gang won the detective agency and its founder widespread acclaim (and convinced many businesses, including large cattle and mining operations, to employ the Pinkerton agency for security and protection). But there were times when the Pinkertons' role as private arbiters of justice became a cause for widespread concern and even outrage.

One incident that provoked public condemnation involved the notorious James Gang. The gang, whose primary members were all former Confederate guerrillas from Missouri—Jesse and Frank James and their cousins Cole, Jim, John, and Bob Younger—began robbing banks shortly after the Civil War. Though the gang would graduate to robbing trains in 1873, by this time the Pinkerton National Detective Agency had already been pursuing them unsuccessfully for five years, having been hired by a bankers' association after a March 1868 bank robbery in Russellville, Kentucky. Like the Renos, the Jameses and Youngers were virtually untouchable in their home territory of Clay County, Missouri, but not simply because neighbors were afraid of them. Loyalty toward these sons of the Confederacy, as well as resentment at the harsh conditions endured by Missourians after the war, ran deep. In some quarters, the gang's criminal activities were even seen as a continuation of the fight against the hated Yankees.

In 1874, within the space of a month, three Pinkerton operatives were killed while pursuing the James Gang. Louis Lull and Joseph Wickher died in a shoot-out that also claimed the life of outlaw John Younger, and John W. Whicher turned up dead by the side of a road after announcing his intentions to capture the James brothers at the farm of their mother, Zerelda Samuels.

Allan Pinkerton exploded when he heard about the deaths of his detectives. In a letter to his agency's general manager, George Bangs, he railed, "I know that the

James and the Youngers are desperate men, and that when we meet it must be the death of one or both of us. . . . [M]y blood was spilt, and they must repay, there is no use talking, they must die."

On the night of January 26, 1875, Pinkerton detectives surrounded the Samuels farmhouse, believing Jesse and Frank James to be inside visiting their mother. The Pinkertons tossed an incendiary device or a bomb through the window, intending, perhaps, to force the occupants out of the house. But when Jesse and Frank James's stepfather pushed the device into the fireplace, it exploded, blowing off part of Zerelda Samuels's arm and killing the Jameses' eight-year-old half-brother, Archie.

After the explosion, the Pinkerton detectives fled, but one of them dropped a revolver stamped with the initials of the agency, making it clear who was responsible for the attack. Outraged citizens excoriated the Pinkertons for their cowardice, and newspapers around the country joined in the criticism. *The Kansas City Times* declared, "[T]here is no crime, however dastardly, which merits a retribution as savage and fiendish as the one which these men acting under the semblance of the law have perpetrated." Allan Pinkerton, it seemed to many people, was carrying out a personal vendetta against the James brothers, and he was using his quasi-official law enforcement status to get away with it. Outrage at this state of affairs led to an attempt to have Pinkerton tried for the murder of Archie Samuels.

But the James debacle wasn't the only reason the public increasingly questioned the power of private detectives in general and of the Pinkertons in particular. As providers of security for big businesses, the Pinkertons were drawn into many volatile labor disputes. And not surprisingly, their pro-business role aroused bitterness, resentment, and suspicion on the part of workers. In 1886 a Pinkerton operative mistakenly shot an innocent bystander during the Chicago stockyard strikes. A year later a young boy was killed by a Pinkerton detective during labor unrest on the Jersey City coal wharves. In 1888, when train engineers for the Burlington Railroad went on strike, more than 50 Pinkerton agents were enlisted as replacement workers—or, in union parlance, "scabs." With no cards left to play, John A. Bauereisen, the head of the Brotherhood of Locomotive Engineers, dynamited railroad property. The Pinkertons promptly arrested him, effectively ending the strike.

The Pinkertons' popularity plummeted. Not only labor union members, but American citizens from all walks of life, believed the detectives were exploiting their power, doing the dirty work of the moneyed business interests that employed them. Such was the general loathing for his private detectives and their anti-labor activities that Allan Pinkerton was spurred to prohibit further Pinkerton involvement in the lawful activities of labor unions. Pinkerton spent much of the rest of his life trying to polish the now-tarnished image of the private detective.

BAIL, BONDSMEN, AND BOUNTY HUNTERS IN EARLY AMERICA

3

To be a bounty hunter in the Wild West, a person needed only toughness, resourcefulness, and a willingness to assume the risk of a sudden, violent death.

Private detectives weren't the only group in 19th-century America for whom pursuing outlaws was a business arrangement rather than an official duty. Especially in the West, bounty hunters also played a prominent role in supplementing official law enforcement.

Unlike private detectives, bounty hunters did not work under a contract. Rather, they were freelancers who made their livings collecting the reward money offered for the capture of certain criminals. They received payment upon turning over to a peace officer a wanted criminal (or the criminal's body, in the case of someone wanted dead or alive). Anyone willing to assume the considerable risk involved could be a bounty hunter. This peculiar niche in frontier law enforcement developed for the same reason that private detectives became so important in the West: there weren't enough sheriffs and marshals, public agents of law enforcement, to cover the vast, sparsely inhabited area.

But the practice of bounty hunting actually originated two centuries earlier and across the Atlantic Ocean from America's Wild West. Conditions in 17th-century England resembled those of the later American frontier. Outside the cities and towns, there existed no official law enforcement. In the countryside and particularly on the open road, crime flourished. Bandits known as highwaymen preyed upon luckless travelers, especially those journeying by coach, who were generally well-to-do.

In 1692, in an effort to curb highway robbery, the English Parliament passed the Highwayman Act. This law offered a reward (or bounty) of £40 to anyone who would capture and prosecute a highway bandit. As in America 200 years later, it was hoped that the generous reward would entice private individuals to do what public law officers could not.

To a certain extent, the law worked as intended. Bounty hunters did come forward to fill the gap in official law enforcement. However, the men attracted to this line of work weren't always the most savory characters. Indeed, many seemed on the verge of outlawry themselves, and the conduct of bounty hunters went largely unmonitored by officials. The story of Jonathan Wild, one of England's first professional bounty hunters, clearly shows the dangers inherent in this sort of arrangement.

Wild, born in Staffordshire around 1683, spent several years as a member of London's criminal underworld before embarking on a career as a bounty hunter. Bestowing upon himself the rather grandiose title of "Thief-taker General of Great Britain and Ireland," Wild collected the bounties on more than 120 bandits over the course of a seven-year career. He also opened a shop that specialized in recovering stolen property for a reward.

It turned out, however, that the "Thief-taker General" was himself a thief. Wild hadn't really been recov-

A highwayman victimizes an unfortunate traveler on a lonely English road. The inability of official law enforcement to deal with crime in the countryside prompted Parliament to pass the Highwayman Act, which created the profession of bounty hunter.

ering stolen property; rather, he'd been getting it from his old criminal connections, with whom he split the fees the original owners paid to get it back. In effect, Wild had set up a fencing operation. Convicted on numerous charges, he received a death sentence and, before an unusually angry crowd that pelted him with dirt and stones, faced the gallows on May 24, 1725.

The same fate would befall Tom Horn, one of 19th-century America's most famous bounty hunters, when he crossed the rather thin line between the legally sanctioned violence of bounty hunting into murder for hire. Besides bounty hunting, Horn's fabled career included stints as a cavalry scout, deputy sheriff, Pinkerton detective, and champion calf-roper.

"Killing men is my specialty," Horn once remarked. "I look at it as a business proposition, and I think I have a corner on the market."

Unfortunately, Horn, like many other American bounty hunters, sometimes forgot the legal basis for his work. In the mid-1890s he signed on as a stock detective with the Wyoming Cattle Growers' Association, headquartered in Cheyenne. His job was to stop cattle rustling.

Rustling had for years been a problem for the Wyoming cattle barons. To build up their stock with no outlay of funds, small ranchers simply stole animals from the enormous herds of the larger operations. Attempts to prosecute rustlers in court had generally proved unsuccessful because juries tended to side with the small entrepreneur trying to eke out a living. Frustrated with the legal system, the cattle barons decided to take matters into their own hands.

As a stock detective, Tom Horn's job description included something at which he had shown himself particularly adept: bounty hunting. Only now it was the cattle interests, not lawmen, that determined who was wanted. And Horn made no attempt to bring anyone in alive. For a bounty of $600 he meticulously tracked the unfortunate rustler, learning the man's habits and waiting for the opportunity to strike. Horn's favorite weapon was a long-distance rifle, and he left the bodies of his victims where they fell, usually on the open range. He placed a large rock under each man's head to signal his employer that he had done the shooting and that the bounty should be paid.

No concrete evidence linked Horn to any of the cattle rustler killings, though the identity of the gunman was an open secret. Anyway, most people couldn't get too upset about the deaths, because the men targeted were thieves and lawbreakers. All that changed on the morning of July 18, 1901.

Horn's target that day was a rancher named Kels Nickell. Following his usual procedure, the gunman dismounted from his horse some three-quarters of a

Tom Horn in prison. In the Wild West, the line between the legally sanctioned violence of bounty hunting and murder for hire could be quite thin. Horn would be hanged in 1903 for crossing that line.

mile from Nickell's cabin, took off his boots so as not to leave footprints, and waited with his Winchester rifle at his side. Horn had studied his quarry's habits for a few days, and he knew that Nickell checked his gate once a day. Unfortunately, on this day Nickell's 14-year-old son Willie was sent to the gate in his father's stead, and the boy wore his father's rain slicker. At 300 yards Horn couldn't tell the difference, and he killed Willie with a shot to the head.

After deputy U.S. marshal Joseph LeFors elicited a drunken confession, Horn was arrested and tried for the killing. He was hanged on November 20, 1903, the day before his 43rd birthday. Tom Horn's demise was emblematic of the fate of bounty hunters in supplementing a public law enforcement system whose officers had been too few and far between to pursue everyone wanted for a crime. When Horn first visited Cheyenne, it was a small frontier town, surrounded by million-acre ranches. When he died, it was a city with automobiles in the streets. With the settlement of the West came all the institutions of "civilized" society, including organized, adequately staffed police forces. A citizenry that more closely resembled the urban middle class than the cowboys of old by and large preferred that the organized police forces catch criminals. Bounty hunters, whose methods tended to be excessively violent and who often flirted with illegality themselves, were no longer needed or wanted.

But the initial capture (or killing) of criminals, the role for which bounty hunters became enshrined in America's frontier myth, was only one aspect of bounty hunting. A more important function—one that remains vital to American criminal justice even today—involved ensuring that accused criminals would be present for their trials.

That sort of bounty hunting also had its origins in an English practice: bail. Sometime before the Norman Conquest of 1066, English sheriffs began releasing certain accused criminals from custody pending their trials. A person called a "surety," usually a friend of the accused, assumed responsibility for making certain that the "principal" (the defendant) appeared to answer the charges against him or her. If the principal didn't show up for trial, the surety could receive the punishment that a conviction on those charges would have brought the principal. Though one might think that such a prospect would have dissuaded most people from assuming the role of surety, medieval English society was tightly knit and not at all mobile. The risks of a defendant fleeing were small.

By the 13th century, a financial obligation had replaced the surety's exposure to punishment. The surety, a well-respected and prosperous member of the community, promised to pay a sum of money or surrender a piece of property if the principal failed to appear before the magistrates. Even though the surety almost always knew the principal personally, the state further lessened his financial risk by empowering him to seize the principal anywhere and at any time, even before the principal had failed to appear for trial. In fact, under English common law (the body of law derived from judicial decisions) bail was viewed as an extension of state imprisonment, and even though he or she had been freed by an official procedure, the criminal suspect was legally considered to be in a state of perpetual escape. A surety thus enjoyed the same, almost unlimited powers in dealing with a principal that a sheriff had in pursuing an escaped prisoner.

After England's American colonies won their independence, the Founding Fathers guaranteed the right of criminal defendants to bail in the Bill of Rights. The Eighth Amendment to the Constitution begins, "Excessive bail shall not be required. . . ." The Judiciary Act of 1789 specified that bail was to be set in all criminal cases "except where the punishment may be death"; in those cases judges on district or circuit courts could decide whether to offer it.

Bail was seen as a fundamental right for at least two reasons. First, it seemed unfair that a person presumed innocent under the law (as are American defendants before they have been convicted in court) should in effect be punished by being incarcerated before his or her trial. And second, by limiting contact with lawyers, incarceration could hamper the accused's ability to prepare an effective defense. (A third, more practical consideration that may not have been on the Founding Fathers' minds is cost. Pretrial detention constitutes a significant expense for the state.)

Bail in the early years of the United States paralleled the system that had evolved in England. Judges would release a defendant awaiting trial into the custody of a "reputable" surety who put up money or property as a guarantee that the defendant would appear for trial. The system worked because most Americans had deep roots in their communities. Sureties and the defendants they vouched for knew one another well. More often than not, judges also knew sureties at least by reputation, so they had a good basis upon which to gauge a surety's trustworthiness.

As the United States grew and society became more mobile, deep personal ties to the community became rarer. Accused criminals began finding it harder to line up sureties who were willing to accept custody of them and who were also deemed trustworthy by the courts.

American entrepreneurs soon recognized a golden opportunity in the plight of these defendants. For a fee (typically a percentage of the bail), a private businessman would post with the court a bond in the full amount of the bail. The businessman, called a bail bondsman, then accepted custody of the defendant until the trial. If the defendant fled and could not be brought back for trial, the bail bondsman forfeited the entire bond. By the mid-1800s the commercial bail-bonding system had replaced the personal surety system almost everywhere.

Two relics from English common law helped shape the wide-ranging authority given to early American bail bondsmen. First, release on bail was considered a continuation of state imprisonment, despite the facts that the principal wasn't physically confined and that a private individual was given responsibility for him or her. Second, though the state sanctioned the bail process, in the eyes of the law the principal was in a state of per-

The Constitutional Convention, 1787. America's Founding Fathers considered bail for criminal defendants a fundamental right and guaranteed it in the Eighth Amendment.

petual escape. Bail bondsmen thus had the power to arrest their clients at any time, in any place, by whatever means they deemed necessary. These were the same powers accorded a sheriff pursuing an escaped prisoner.

Most bail-bonding businesses in the 1800s were small operations, often run by a single entrepreneur. Bondsmen couldn't personally locate and bring in all their clients before trials, so they hired independent contractors—bounty hunters—to do the job for them.

Three influential 19th-century legal cases delineated the considerable power of bounty hunters. The first case, called *Nicolls v. Ingersoll*, was decided in 1810 by the New York Supreme Court. After being arrested in Connecticut, Nicolls engaged a commercial bail bondsman to post his $500 bail. He then traveled to his home in New York. Nervous that his client was in a different state, the bondsman hired a bounty hunter to seize Nicolls and haul him back to Connecticut—*before* his scheduled trial. The bounty hunter carried out this task by breaking into Nicolls's house at midnight and forcibly subduing him.

Nicolls filed a lawsuit for trespass, false imprisonment, and assault, and the case ended up before the New York Supreme Court. The court threw out Nicolls's suit, finding that the bounty hunter, as the authorized agent of the bail bondsman, had the same rights of arrest as the bondsman. This meant that he could legally arrest the principal "at all times and in all places"—even if that meant breaking into the principal's house in the middle of the night, even if the principal hadn't yet failed to show up in court. The court stated that the bounty hunter's power stemmed not from any judicial process but from the private contract between the bail bondsman and the principal.

Sixty-two years after the *Nicolls* decision, the United States Supreme Court reaffirmed the broad rights of bounty hunters in the case of *Taylor v. Taintor*. "When bail is given," the Court stated,

> the principal is regarded as delivered to the custody of his sureties. Their dominion is a continuance of the original imprisonment. Whenever they choose to do so, they may seize him and deliver him up [to the court]; and if that cannot be done at once, they may imprison him until it can be done. They may exercise their rights in person or by agent. They may pursue him into another State; may arrest him on the Sabbath; and . . . may break and enter his home for that purpose. The seizure is not made by virtue of new process. None is needed. It is likened to the rearrest by the sheriff of an escaping prisoner.

The *Taylor* decision confirmed that bounty hunters held greater powers of arrest with fewer restrictions than the police. To arrest a suspect not in the act of committing a crime, police generally needed a warrant, and custom dictated that they not make the arrest on Sunday. To transport a prisoner across state lines, police had to obtain extradition papers. No such limitations were placed on bounty hunters, who could seize a principal whenever they wanted and use deadly force if necessary.

In 1898 a Pennsylvania circuit court decision, *In re Von Der Ahe*, made it clear that persons released on bail could not look to the Constitution for protection against the excesses of bounty hunters. A bounty hunter working for a Pennsylvania bail bondsman had arrested Von Der Ahe at his home in Missouri and taken him back to Pennsylvania before his trial there. Von Der Ahe questioned the constitutionality of the arrest, claiming that because it had been made without the authorization of any legal proceeding, his Fifth Amendment right to due process had been violated. The circuit court disagreed. It ruled that the Constitution placed no limits on a bounty hunter's right to arrest a principal, because the bounty hunter was not acting as an agent of the state. Rather, he was merely enforcing a private contract. In hiring the bondsman to post his bail bond, the court ruled, Von Der Ahe had implicitly given his consent to being arrested whenever and however the bondsman or his bounty hunter deemed appropriate.

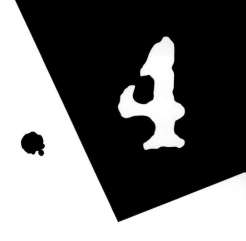

REPOSSESSING HUMAN BEINGS

On July 18, 1994, Jrae Mason sat on the stoop of her Harlem residence enjoying the warm summer evening. Mason, a grandmother of 13, was waiting for a friend to stop by.

Two people eventually did stop by, but they weren't friends. The two men grabbed Mason, twisted her arms behind her back, handcuffed her, and dragged her into her apartment. There they announced that she would soon be taking a ride—to Alabama. Thus began one woman's nightmarish journey into the world of modern-day bounty hunting.

Although many Americans are unaware of their existence, let alone the important role they play in the justice system, an estimated 10,000 bounty hunters ply their trade in the United States today. Many are themselves ex-convicts, yet according to attorney and bounty hunting expert Jonathan Drimmer, "they enjoy broader powers than police officers, they are unlicensed, unregulated, and generally free from constitu-

Bail agent Josh Herman, holding the rap sheet of a client who has just failed to appear for a court date, talks by cell phone with an associate. Unless a bounty hunter can find and arrest the bail jumper within a specified time, Herman will forfeit the bail bond he posted with the court.

Martin Tong shows a scar on his wrist, the result of an encounter with two bounty hunters who broke into his apartment and shot him three times. The fugitive the bounty hunters were seeking had moved from Tong's apartment the previous year.

tional constraints."

American society and criminal justice have undergone dramatic changes in the 20th century, but the bounty hunter is essentially a holdover from the 1800s. In his article "When Man Hunts Man: The Rights and Duties of Bounty Hunters in the American Criminal Justice System," Drimmer states:

> The rights and powers of . . . bounty hunters have changed little since the nineteenth century. Courts still view release on bail as a continuation of the defendant's original imprisonment, and a bounty hunter's arrest as an extension of the state's initial capture. Bounty hunters still possess broad rights to search for and arrest defendants, whom courts continue to view as in a state of perpetual escape.

And courts still follow the precedent of the 19th-century legal decisions holding that the search and arrest rights of bounty hunters originate in a private contract and thus are not matters of constitutional concern to the state. This despite the obvious benefits the state reaps from the private bail system in general and bounty hunters in particular.

Although some defendants are released before trial under various public, tax-funded bail arrangements; are freed after personally posting 10 percent of the bail amount in cash; or are released on a so-called personal recognizance bond requiring them to put up no money unless they fail to appear in court, the majority of crime suspects turn to private bail (or bonding) agents to secure their pretrial release. (The term *bondsmen* is falling out of favor, in large part because some 45 percent of the people in this job are women.) Bail saves the state considerable money. The average cost of keeping a person behind bars was estimated at $1,600 per month in 1994, and the average length of time between arrest and sentencing in felony cases was about eight months. On average, then, bail can save the state nearly $13,000 per defendant. It also relieves overcrowding in the nation's jail systems.

The vast majority of those released under bail arrangements of all types—an estimated 88 to 95 percent—show up for their court dates. When a defendant does jump bail, however, someone has to find and retrieve him or her. Bounty hunters do a much better job of this than the police. In part because of budgetary restraints, the police catch no more than 92 percent of public-bail fugitives (some estimates put the rate as low as 73 percent). In contrast, bounty hunters—or, as many prefer to be called, skip tracers or fugitive-recovery agents—return an estimated 99.2 percent of those who skip out on bail agents. This remarkable success rate is due in no small measure to bounty hunters' financial incentive: they are paid (generally 10 percent of the bond amount) only when they catch the fugitive.

Bounty hunters capture some 25,000 to 30,000 bail jumpers each year in the United States. Jrae Mason, the Harlem grandmother, was not one of them. Javier Mulinary and Darren Fuentes, the two bounty hunters who snatched Mason on that summer night in 1994, believed her to be a woman named Audrey White Smith who had jumped bail in Alabama. Mason insisted she had never even been to Alabama and showed the bounty hunters several forms of identification to prove she was not the woman they wanted. Nevertheless, Mulinary and Fuentes delivered Mason to two associates, Wally Holliman and Robert Hall Jr.

Holliman and Hall shackled Mason's ankles, loaded her into a car, and set off for Alabama. When their prisoner repeatedly tried to tell them that this was a case of mistaken identity, the bounty hunters told her to shut up or they would throw her in the trunk. Mason later reported thinking she was going to die.

More than three days after her ordeal began in Harlem, it ended at Alabama's Tuscaloosa County Jail. There officials noticed that the prisoner the bounty hunters wanted to turn over bore little resemblance to the fugitive Audrey White Smith. In fact, Mason stood five inches taller and weighed 40 pounds more. Further checking revealed that Mason was indeed who she claimed to be. Eventually the bounty hunters put her on a bus for New York City.

As harrowing as her ordeal was, Jrae Mason fared

better than other people mistakenly targeted by bounty hunters. In Kansas City in 1997, for example, two bounty hunters broke into the apartment of Martin Tong and shot him in the leg, wrist, and ear; the bail jumper the men were looking for had moved from the apartment the previous year. In Houston two years earlier, a pregnant woman named Betty Caballero suffered a miscarriage after a beating inflicted by a bounty hunter who mistook her for a bail jumper he was seeking. Two other bounty hunters who got the wrong man beat up a high school student in Memphis, Tennessee, in 1998. In still another case of mistaken identity, a firefighter named Pamela Read saw her dream vacation to Disneyland turn into a nightmare when a bounty hunter kicked down the door of her motel room. As her terrified children watched, the bounty hunter held a cocked gun to Read's head and accused her of being a prostitute who had skipped bail.

But the conduct of bounty hunters has recently been called into question in more than just cases of mistaken identity. Some bounty hunters have used what most people would consider excessive force in subduing fugitives. In 1994, for example, bounty hunters repeatedly kicked a bail jumper while he was handcuffed and then extracted his gold tooth with a pair of pliers. That same year, another bounty hunter hung a suspect upside down in his car during a trip of several hundred miles. In 1987 a bounty hunter in Phoenix, Arizona, provoked outrage when he fatally shot an unarmed bail jumper, Richard Bachellor, in the back while Bachellor was walking with his wife and three-year-old son. (As in the days of the Wild West, bounty hunters get paid—and bail agents recover their bond—whether the quarry is dead or alive. They must either deliver the bail jumper or a death certificate to the court within a specified time.)

In addition to complaints about their use of excessive violence, bounty hunters have been assailed for

Chris Foote and Spring Wright, a young couple killed in their bedroom when five masked men claiming to be bounty hunters stormed into a Phoenix, Arizona, house and a gunfight ensued.

tactics that seem unfair, such as forcibly detaining and interrogating—sometimes at gunpoint and for extended periods—friends or family members of bail jumpers in order to learn a fugitive's whereabouts. One bounty hunter incapacitated an innocent blind man with pepper spray so that he could make an arrest without the man getting in the way. Another sprayed two children of a fugitive with Mace for the same reason.

And sheer carelessness on the part of bounty hunters also results in considerable harm to innocent bystanders. In 1998, for example, two bounty hunters attempting to make an arrest in Los Angeles shot bystander David Villanueva in the chest.

Bail agents and bounty hunters insist—and a close look at the facts bears them out—that outrageous conduct is the exception in fugitive recovery. Longtime bounty hunters say that the best way to bring in a bail jumper is by reasoning with him or her; many claim

they have never pulled a gun or kicked in a door.

Still, some incidents of serious violence are virtually guaranteed, given the nature of the work. Some felons are extremely dangerous and have no qualms about using deadly force to avoid facing trial, and bounty hunters as well as bail jumpers have been killed during attempted arrests.

But perhaps a more significant factor in the level of violence associated with bounty hunting is the wide latitude given to bounty hunters, combined with a lack of regulation. In most of the country, licensing requirements for bounty hunters are nonexistent. This means that virtually any adult can call himself or herself a bounty hunter and can, in the pursuit of a bail jumper, break and enter a private home and use all necessary force to subdue the suspect. Despite their authority to use deadly force if required, bounty hunters need not— and for the most part, do not—receive any formal train-

Self-proclaimed bounty hunter Michael Sanders at his arraignment for the killings of Chris Foote and Spring Wright. Sanders, who fired 18 shots from his assault rifle into Foote and Wright's bedroom, was eventually convicted of first-degree murder.

ing in the use of force. This sets them apart from police officers, who are required to receive such training.

Other legal and procedural checks on police behavior do not apply to bounty hunters. These checks include the requirement that, under most circumstances, police obtain a warrant to arrest a suspect not currently engaged in the commission of a crime. In obtaining the warrant, the police must demonstrate probable cause for believing the suspect will be in a particular place. This limits the chances that the wrong house will be searched and the wrong person arrested. In addition, the police must identify themselves and, unless there is a compelling reason otherwise, must serve warrants during the day. This limits the risk of accidental violence, a risk that increases enormously when bounty hunters—as is their prerogative—break into a home in the middle of the night and confront startled and frightened occupants, who often believe, not unreasonably, that the intruders are criminals. To transport a suspect across state lines, police, unlike bounty hunters, must go through the process of extradition, which involves a court hearing. Extradition procedures would have prevented the harrowing interstate odyssey of Jrae Mason.

In the wake of recent mishaps and abuses such as the Jrae Mason case, calls for curbs on the powers of bounty hunters have sounded from various quarters. At the root of these calls is the sense that the system unnecessarily promotes violence and simply conflicts with common sense. Lawyers, journalists, and victims of mistaken identity all have asked why the government regulates the activities of, for example, debt collectors more than those of people who are authorized to use deadly force. Both groups are private actors. After what seemed like a particularly flagrant case of bounty hunter abuse in August 1997, attorney Gary Klahr observed, "[I]t's harder now to repossess a car—you're supposed to alert the police first—than it is to repossess a human being."

As it turned out, the incident to which Klahr was referring didn't involve real bounty hunters, as initial media reports had indicated. Nevertheless, it spoke volumes about the nature of bounty hunting in America.

At 4 A.M. on a Sunday morning, five men in ski masks smashed through the door of a Phoenix, Arizona, house with a sledgehammer. In one bedroom, the heavily armed intruders found three children ages 6, 11, and 12 and their mother, whom they handcuffed and beat on the head with a flashlight. While one of the men held the family at gunpoint, the others proceeded to search the rest of the house. In another bedroom were Chris Foote, a 23-year-old construction worker, and his girlfriend, Spring Wright, a 19-year-old college student. When the masked men kicked down the bedroom door, Foote apparently fired at them with his handgun, touching off a gunfight. Foote managed to wound two of the intruders, but a hail of bullets killed him and Wright in their bed. The intruders had come prepared for a battle: two wore body armor, and at least one had an assault rifle, from which he fired 18 rounds into the bedroom.

When police apprehended the men, they said they were bounty hunters, and they carried papers that indicated they were looking for a California bail jumper. Because the fugitive had no connection to the Phoenix house, it appeared to be another unfortunate case of bounty hunters going to the wrong home. But as they looked further into the case, investigators found that the pieces just didn't add up. The California case was five years old, and the bail jumper in question was no longer being sought. Moreover, the bail bonding company the men claimed to be working for had never hired—or even heard of—them.

Investigators came to believe that robbery was the real reason for the predawn raid. The men had apparently concocted the bounty hunting story to protect themselves from prosecution in the event something went wrong. That the plan might have worked struck

Surrounded by family and friends of Chris Foote and Spring Wright, Arizona governor Jane Hull signs into law a bill requiring that bounty hunters in the state be licensed and that they get permission from occupants before entering a home. Ironically, investigators believe that the men who killed Foote and Wright were actually robbers posing as bounty hunters.

many citizens as a powerful indictment of the wide latitude given bounty hunters under the law.

For their part, police officers have questioned why bounty hunters aren't bound by the same constitutional rules regarding searches and the treatment of suspects as are public law enforcement agents. The Fourth Amendment prohibits police from searching a home, under most circumstances, without a warrant or the consent of the occupants. Bounty hunters, on the other hand, can break into a suspect's home (or even the home of a third party, if they believe the suspect is there), and anyone who interferes with such a search can be held criminally liable. Upon arresting suspects, police must also give them Miranda warnings (informing them of their right to remain silent, of their right to have legal counsel during questioning, and of the fact that any statements they do make could be used against them in court). Failure to do so renders inadmissible any evidence or confession the suspect gives. By contrast, bounty hunters need not Mirandize suspects, and in fact, confessions they obtain through coercion are still admissible in court.

Even some of the very people who employ bounty hunters—bail agents—have recently called for changes. In testimony before the House Judiciary Committee's Subcommittee on the Constitution in March 1998, Armando Roche, president of the Professional Bail Agents of the United States, declared, "In short, the position of the professional bail agents is clear: regulate the bounty hunters at the state level or prohibit bounty hunters altogether."

The prospect of a complete ban on bounty hunting is extremely remote. States simply benefit too much from the current arrangement: at no cost to taxpayers, they can release prisoners before trial, thus saving considerable expenses on detention. And given bounty hunters' proficiency in locating fugitives, states have a greater than 99 percent assurance that suspects will be returned for trial. Indeed, states have an interest in seeing that bounty hunters not only stay in business but also retain their broad authority. For it is largely this authority that enables bounty hunters to achieve such a high rate of success in capturing bail jumpers.

Critics such as Jonathan Drimmer believe that states can both allow bounty hunters to retain the broad powers they need to capture fugitives and protect citizens from "the increasingly frequent violence that bounty hunters inflict on the public at large." But first, Drimmer believes, courts must abandon the "legal fiction" that bounty hunters are merely private actors enforcing private contracts. It is this legal interpretation, dating from the 19th century, that has prevented constitutional standards from being applied to the conduct of bounty hunters. In Drimmer's view, bail agents and bounty hunters work so closely with the state—and have the same interests as the state—that they must be considered de facto, or actual, state actors. Indeed, in some respects, bounty hunters' activities are already directed by the state. For example, in many states the forfeiture of a bail bond does not absolve bail agents and bounty hunters from legal responsibility; they are actually *required* to try to recover fugitives.

If the courts did redefine bounty hunters as state actors, all the constitutional restrictions on police conduct could apply to them as well. Bounty hunters would need a warrant to search a private home. Confessions and evidence they obtained in violation of the Fourth and Fifth Amendments would be inadmissible. And no longer could they arrest suspects *before* they had failed to appear in court under the absurd rationale that people released on bail are in a perpetual state of escape. In short, as Jonathan Drimmer explains, people released on bail, "like other citizens whom the law assumes are innocent of a crime, . . . [would] enjoy the full panoply of rights guaranteed by the Constitution."

In the absence of court decisions redefining the status of bounty hunters, lawmakers have begun to explore legislative solutions to the problem of rogue conduct in fugitive recovery. The Citizen Protection Act, introduced in Congress in 1998, would make bounty hunters who committed civil rights violations subject to the same federal criminal and civil penalties that apply to police officers guilty of similar violations. Illinois, Kentucky, Oregon, and Wisconsin have passed laws requiring out-of-state bounty hunters to obtain court orders from local judges to arrest fugitives. Arizona now requires bounty hunters to be licensed and to receive permission before entering a house. Texas makes bounty hunters get arrest warrants and execute them in the presence of peace officers or licensed private investigators. And various individuals and groups have proposed legislation requiring that all bounty hunters be licensed and certified in the states in which they work. (Bail agents already have strict licensing and certification requirements.)

Among those who believe that the problems with bounty hunting can largely be eliminated by weeding out the abusive and the ill-prepared few are the Professional Bail Agents of the United States and the University of Southern Mississippi. Together they launched the nation's first comprehensive training and certification program for bounty hunters. "We want to kick out the cowboys," declared criminal justice professor William B. Taylor, who was involved in setting up the program. Certification is awarded upon passing a psychological screening exam and completing 84 hours of course work that includes self-defense tactics, confrontation avoidance, ethics, law, and liability.

Although organizers of the Professional Bail Agents of the United States/University of Southern Mississippi program believe their work can spur greater professionalism in fugitive recovery, simple economics might ultimately prove to be a more significant factor. Jrae Mason won $1.2 million in a lawsuit against the bounty hunters who abducted her and the bonding agency that hired them. Another jury awarded Pamela Read, the woman mistaken for a prostitute in California, $1.5 million. It is doubtful that bail agents or the companies that insure them will continue to tolerate bounty hunter misconduct if the price of that misconduct continues to be so high.

IMAGES AND REALITY: THE PRIVATE EYE IN POPULAR CULTURE

Humphrey Bogart as Sam Spade, the archetypal hard-boiled detective, in The Maltese Falcon (1941). Although detective fiction and films are popular worldwide, American audiences seem most enthralled by the hard-boiled genre's gritty depictions of violence and its streetwise, cynical heroes.

Despite some well-publicized recent cases, in the minds of most Americans the image of bounty hunters remains frozen in time. The popular, though erroneous, belief is that bounty hunters faded away with the disappearance of the Wild West. Not so the private eye. From the days of Allan Pinkerton to the present, private investigators have remained in the public spotlight. Or more precisely, perhaps, they have found an enduring place in the public imagination—for most of what we think we know about private investigators comes from fictional representations: detective novels and short stories, motion pictures, TV shows.

As depictions of what being a private investigator is really like, these sources, taken as a whole, may leave something to be desired. One obvious reason is that a detective story, like any other form of popular culture, must entertain an audience. Otherwise, people won't waste their time or money on it. Thus the detective sto-

American author Edgar Allan Poe. Poe is credited with writing the first pure detective story, "The Murders in the Rue Morgue," published in 1841.

ries that are published and filmed invariably have intricate plots replete with mystery, danger, and glamour. Yet the work of the typical private investigator is likely to be quite mundane most of the time. Unfortunately, sitting in a car for hours waiting to photograph a philandering husband and his lover as they emerge from a motel room doesn't form the stuff of great entertainment. "The real-life private eye," observed the acclaimed detective writer Raymond Chandler, "is a sleazy little drudge . . . , a strong-arm guy with no more personality than a black-jack. He has about as much moral stature as a stop-and-go-sign." One might legitimately take exception with Chandler's blanket characterization of private eyes (interestingly, he never worked as one), but he offered the observation to explain why his characters and stories were inherently unrealistic.

This is not to suggest that private investigators never have fascinating cases. But the cumulative effect of fictional depictions is the impression that being a private eye is far more exciting than it really is.

If detective stories by and large don't present a realistic view of private investigators, they do reveal much about society. Their longevity (the genre dates back more than 150 years) and popularity attest to our deep-seated fascination with criminal behavior and with people who confront and expose that behavior. Moreover, detective fiction seems to fulfill another deep-seated desire: the desire to see wrongdoers brought to justice.

Literary scholars cite Edgar Allan Poe's "The Murders in the Rue Morgue," published in 1841, as the first pure detective story. An American, Poe invented a French amateur detective, C. Auguste Dupin, and set his story in Paris, a city that provided a seductive backdrop for the crime: the grisly killing of a woman and her daughter. Dupin solved the case, which had baffled the plodding Paris police, by practicing "headwork" rather than "legwork." He brilliantly used deductive reasoning, drawing logical conclusions about the unknown aspects of the case from information that was known. Such were his powers of logic that he didn't even have to leave the confines of his home.

In 1887 a fictional sleuth who had much in common with Poe's Dupin made his first appearance in *A Study in Scarlet*. Sherlock Holmes, the violin-playing, opium-smoking creation of English writer Sir Arthur

Conan Doyle, would become the most famous fictional detective ever. Like Dupin, Holmes uses pure head-work, but his powers of observation and deductive logic eclipse those of his French predecessor. In a story titled "The Red-Headed League," for example, Holmes deduces that his client was once a manual laborer, takes snuff, is a Freemason, and has been in China—simply by looking at him. As with Dupin before him, Holmes regularly outshines the bumbling police (and his trust-worthy but pedestrian partner, Dr. Watson) because they overlook the significance of the evidence, where-as he truly *sees*. Part of the appeal of Sherlock Holmes and other "classical" detectives (those who rely on observation and deduction alone) is that the reader can, in effect, match wits with the master. In well-writ-ten stories, the necessary clues are provided, and we get to see whether we are perceptive like the hero—or slow-witted like the police.

But not every writer of detective fiction favored Poe's or Conan Doyle's emphasis on reasoning. "Your private detective," declared an American writer who wanted to appeal to his American audience, "does not want to be an erudite solver of riddles in the Sherlock Holmes manner; he wants to be a hard and shifty fel-low, able to take care of himself in any situation, able to get the best of anybody he comes in contact with, whether criminal, innocent by-stander or client." The writer, Dashiell Hammett, was a former Pinkerton agent who became one of the earliest and best practi-tioners of the "hard-boiled" school of detective fiction. Emerging after World War I, the hard-boiled detective was a distinctly American creation.

America had been consuming detective fiction voraciously since the 1870s. While Pinkerton opera-tives tracked bandits across the wide spaces of the law-less West, fictional private detectives roamed the pages of countless dime novels (books of 16 to 32 pages that were printed on the cheapest wood pulp paper and cost just 10 cents). Allan Pinkerton himself was one of the earliest dime-novel chroniclers of the American detective. Following a stroke in 1868, Pinkerton began dictating his adventures to a ghostwriter, who fleshed out the tales. His first book, *The Expressman and the Detective*, sold 15,000 copies within 60 days of its publication in 1875. Fifteen more Pinkerton dime novels followed over the next 10 years.

Dime-novel detective stories sold like nothing else, and their simple, formulaic structure—crime, suspense, capture, and punishment—enabled writers to churn them out at a rapid pace. Little effort was expended on characterization, and the hundreds of fictional detectives that appeared, in every city from Boston to San Francisco and throughout the Wild West, tended to blur together. Often, writers tried to distinguish their characters simply by giving them a particular hobby or job. Significantly, violence tended to be depicted in a cartoonish manner.

In keeping with Americans' prevailing self-image, the dime-novel detectives were rugged individualists—courageous, strong, and honest. They upheld the law when the government failed. Their motives were beyond reproach. Just as the dime novel served as many Easterners' primary source of information about the West, it shaped many readers' ideas about real private detectives. In readers' minds, these men (and to a lesser extent, women) were genuine American heroes.

Writers of hard-boiled detective fiction, a style that later came to dominate the market—and that remains influential today—added a certain ambivalence to the public's perceptions of private eyes. Not that it was a case of art completely transforming the audience, however. America had already lost much of its innocence on the bloody battlefields of World War I. Unalloyed heroes and cartoonish depictions of violence were hard to swallow after the carnage in Europe.

Writers of hard-boiled fiction sought to depict vio-

Hard-boiled private eye plus beautiful, deceptive client equals silver-screen success. Here: Jack Nicholson and Faye Dunaway in the Academy Award–winning Chinatown (1974).

lence and crime, particularly crime in the cities, more realistically than did their dime-novel predecessors. The detectives who inhabit these books exist in a sordid world of corruption, danger, and violence. Constant exposure to urban evils has eliminated in them all traces of softness and sentimentality—as hard-boiling an egg makes it tough inside and out. The hard-boiled detective is nobody's fool: streetwise, cynical, and jaded, he is concerned, first and foremost, with looking out for himself. This he does quite well, when necessary through violent means, which are depicted graphically. Morally, the hard-boiled detective can be an ambiguous figure. He is certainly not a paragon of virtue. Sometimes operating at the margins of legality, he frequently runs afoul of the police, who are often corrupt and, true to the precedent set by Poe's Dupin stories and Conan Doyle's Sherlock Holmes tales, incompetent. Yet in many acclaimed hard-boiled detective stories, the protagonist emerges as a person of integrity because he adheres to a personal code. More than the groundbreaking depictions of violence, it is perhaps this moral element—which the hero clings to in the midst of pervasive cynicism, seediness, and corruption—that formed the basis for the huge popularity of hard-boiled stories.

Dashiell Hammett introduced one of the genre's most famous characters, the private eye Sam Spade, in his 1930 novel *The Maltese Falcon*. Spade, a tough, cynical loner, becomes mixed up with a group of unsavory characters trying to get their hands on a jewel-studded statue. Clever, if not brilliant like Sherlock Holmes, he solves the case by means of his toughness and his vast backlog of experience. He has, the reader senses, seen it all before.

Although the book met with critical and financial success, it was as a motion picture that *The Maltese Falcon* became most famous. Actually, the story was filmed three times—in 1931, 1936, and 1941—but the 1941 version, directed by John Huston and starring Humphrey Bogart as Sam Spade, stands out as a classic. In this version, Spade bests villains played by Sydney Greenstreet and Peter Lorre and falls in love with his client, a rather mercenary beauty played by Mary Astor. Despite his feelings for the femme fatale, he eventually turns her in for the murder of his partner, Miles, even though he had detested Miles. His code of conduct, as he explains at the end of the film, dictates that a detective look out for his partner, regardless of personal feelings, regardless of the consequences.

The Maltese Falcon enthralled audiences, garnered praise from the critics (along with two Academy Award nominations), and showed moviemakers the silver-screen potential of hard-boiled detective stories. These stories translated particularly well into a popular motion-picture genre called film noir—a French term meaning "black film," which refers to the movies' abundant use of night scenes and shadowy lighting, as well as to their focus on dark themes such as crime.

Of the many hard-boiled detective movies that followed *The Maltese Falcon*, among the darkest—and best—are *The Big Sleep* (1946) and *Chinatown* (1974). In the former, Humphrey Bogart once again brought a popular literary detective to the movie screen: Raymond Chandler's tough but honorable private eye Philip Marlowe. *The Big Sleep* concerns Marlowe's efforts to find a missing person—and solve a series of murders—an effort complicated by the deceptions of his client, a wealthy and beautiful woman (played by Lauren Bacall), and her dysfunctional family. *Chinatown*, whose complicated plot involves water rights, land grabbing, and murder, takes place in 1930s Los Angeles. As in *The Big Sleep*, its protagonist, private detective Jake Gittes (played by Jack Nicholson), must sift through layers of deception, much of it introduced by his beautiful client (played by Faye Dunaway). Her family is *truly* dysfunctional: as Gittes discovers, she has had a daughter from an incestuous relationship with her father.

Detective fiction and film are wonderfully varied and embrace far more than the hard-boiled style, however. Ross Macdonald, one of the most literate of American detective writers, created a private investigator who actually disliked violence and who was motivated by compassion for people in trouble. That character, Lew Archer, appeared in a series of well-received books beginning with 1949's *The Moving Target*, later adapted for the screen as *Harper* (1966), starring Paul Newman. John MacDonald's hero Travis McGee, a Florida private investigator, blended the hard-boiled and the compassionate in a series of detective novels that incorporated colors in their titles.

More recently, writers and filmmakers have paid

Denzel Washington (right) as private eye Easy Rawlins in 1995's Devil in a Blue Dress.

some attention to diversity in fictional private detection. For example, Sara Paretsky has written a series of novels about a female Chicago private investigator named V. I. Warshawski. In contrast to such fictional female sleuths of the past as British writer Agatha Christie's Jane Marple, who solved crimes in the classical Sherlock Holmes tradition, Warshawski is tough and somewhat hard-boiled. And Walter Mosley brought an African-American point of view to the detective novel through his character Easy Rawlins. Actor Denzel Washington portrayed the Los Angeles private eye in the popular 1995 motion picture *Devil in a Blue Dress*.

In addition to countless appearances in books and motion pictures, the private investigator has been a sta-

Private investigators of all varieties have been a staple not just of American motion pictures but also of American television. Pictured here are Farrah Fawcett (left) and Jaclyn Smith, who played P.I.'s in the hit 1970s series Charlie's Angels.

ple of American television, underscoring America's ongoing fascination with this profession. During the 1950–51 television season, the medium's infancy, 2 of the 20 most popular shows dealt with private eyes. *Martin Kane, Private Eye* and *Man Against Crime* both chronicled the cases of New York detectives. Among the most popular shows of the 1960s was *77 Sunset Strip*, about Hollywood private investigators. In the 1970s, all of the following detective series cracked the annual list of the 20 most popular TV shows: *Mannix*, dealing with a Los Angeles private eye; *Cannon*, whose title detective was gruff and corpulent; *Barnaby Jones*, about an aging private investigator and his young partner; *The Rockford Files*, whose title character was an ex-con who became a private eye; and *Charlie's Angels*, about a private detective agency staffed by three comely female investigators. Among the top-rated shows of the 1980s were *Magnum, P.I.*, about a Vietnam vet–turned–private investigator in Hawaii; *Simon & Simon*, which followed the cases of two brothers who co-owned a private detective business; *Murder, She Wrote*, about a mystery writer and amateur sleuth in the classical detective tradition; *Riptide*, about two California private eyes aided by their computer-genius friend; and *Moonlighting*, about an offbeat detective agency. In the 1990s, private eye shows figured less prominently among viewers' favorites, although *Murder, She Wrote* stayed in the top 10 through mid-decade and the networks continued to introduce new private detective series through the 1998–99 programming year.

The popularity of detective fiction, movies, and television series is a worldwide phenomenon, and the variety of the detective genre is astounding. Classical detectives in the mold of Sherlock Holmes, who use their powers of deduction to solve cases, still flourish. Also popular are procedural detectives, who show more determination than brilliance, doggedly following investigative procedures until they arrive at the truth. But in the United States, perhaps more than anywhere else, fictional detectives in the hard-boiled tradition reign. Americans—in keeping with a national self-image that continues to elevate rugged individualism—favor the man of action, the detective who can take care of himself in a fight and who doesn't shy away from inflicting some mayhem with his fists or his pistol.

THE MANY ROLES OF PRIVATE INVESTIGATORS

T he image of a typical private eye exchanging punches or gunshots with criminals may be a myth, but private detectives do perform a wide variety of investigative and security tasks in the United States. To a certain extent, the scope of their work is easier to outline by describing what private investigators *aren't*, which in essence amounts to contrasting them with police detectives.

As public agents of law enforcement, police detectives, who investigate criminal violations of the law, work for no individual in particular, but for the government. The services of private investigators (P.I.'s), on the other hand, are for hire by any private citizen, and much of their work involves noncriminal matters that

Private investigator Christopher Rush (right), in court with a lawyer and his client. P.I.'s perform a variety of important tasks on behalf of defense lawyers, including conducting independent investigations, finding witnesses, and serving subpoenas.

the police do not investigate or do not assign a high priority to investigating. Examples include documenting marital infidelity, locating missing persons when no evidence of foul play exists, and protecting businesses from potential corporate espionage. A police detective, by obtaining a court warrant, can have a suspect's phone tapped, search his or her residence, or make an arrest. Though some clients may believe otherwise, a private investigator can do none of these things. The only time a P.I. can make an arrest is when he or she witnesses the commission of a felony. (The authority to make a citizen's arrest is granted to all Americans under those circumstances.)

Though surveillance forms a large part of many private investigators' work, legally a P.I. cannot invade a person's privacy by physically searching his or her residence or by means of electronic surveillance, photographing activities behind closed doors, or bugging rooms. Practically speaking, this means that all surveillance must be conducted from public spaces and be confined to activities that occur within public view. Rather than providing an exhilarating day of chasing and shadowing, surveillance work is often tedious and requires long hours and a lot of patience from the P.I. A typical surveillance assignment might involve sitting in a parked car all night, watching a house out of which no one has emerged for hours.

In 1994 there were an estimated 55,000 private detectives in the United States. About 12,000 were self-employed, and almost 15,000 more worked for detective agencies such as Pinkerton's and Burns'. About 18,000 worked as store detectives in department and clothing stores, their primary duties being to prevent shoplifting and employee theft. The rest of these detectives worked for hotels, industry, and other businesses, fulfilling various security and investigative duties.

No national standards govern the licensing of private investigators, and state requirements vary widely.

Minnesota, for example, requires 6,000 hours of experience with a private detective firm; Oregon once licensed a 12-year-old. In certain states a background check, a written exam, and some training are required. In other states the prospective P.I. must merely pay a licensing fee. And some states don't license private investigators at all. This lack of consistent standards is, in the opinion of some experts, quite problematic. Lake Headley, a longtime private detective whom renowned prosecutor Vincent Bugliosi called "the greatest p.i. in the world," spoke in surprisingly critical tones about the overall state of his profession. "I can categorically state," Headley wrote in his book *Vegas P.I.*,

> that with few exceptions people will be happier, richer, and generally better off if they stay away from private investigators. Until recently most states demanded no requirements whatever from a person wanting to become a licensed p.i., and even today the regulations are laughably lax. In some states all that is needed is the purchase of a business license. The field is wide open for hustlers, con men, adventurers, quick-buck artists, incompetents, and other unsavory characters. The bottom line is that with a modicum of creative initiative the average individual can learn what he or she is paying the p.i. to uncover.

This last statement underscores the fact that much P.I. work is routine and procedural, requiring no special skills. For example, a search of public documents, which are available to anyone, is frequently all that is necessary to locate a missing person. And in many cases a woman who suspects her husband of infidelity can confirm her suspicions without photographs or videotape of him in a compromising situation.

On the other hand, private investigators do perform specialized work. From the perspective of the criminal justice system, among the most important of this work is investigation on behalf of defense lawyers.

Before a criminal suspect is brought to trial, police detectives and prosecutors gather evidence—physical

Above: Don Bolles, investigative reporter for the Arizona Republic. Facing page: Phoenix police detectives examine Bolles's car, destroyed by the car bomb that killed him.

evidence as well as witness testimony—to construct a picture of the crime. The picture always supports the conclusion that the defendant committed the crime; otherwise the case would not be brought. But that doesn't necessarily mean that police and prosecutors have turned up all the relevant evidence or that the evidence they have found cannot support a different conclusion.

In essence the defense attorney's job boils down to finding reasons why the jury should believe an alternative version or at least doubt the prosecution's version of the crime. To assist them in this task, many defense lawyers, particularly those whose clients are facing serious charges (and can afford additional expenses), hire private investigators. A P.I. might conduct his or her own investigation of the crime, critically examining the evidence, searching for and interviewing witnesses, and serving subpoenas, legal documents requiring someone to testify about a case. Essentially this is the same work that police detectives do in investigating a crime.

"Much of the work I did over the years came from defense attorneys," Lake Headley revealed, "and I likened my job to that of a hod carrier. I tried to bring lawyers the bricks with which they could construct a solid defense."

Using a different metaphor, Philadelphia P.I. Edward Geigert, a former city police detective, described his work as a defense investigator to a newspaper reporter. "Some cases," he said, "are just airtight for the [prosecution]. But if there are cracks, you have got to see where the light comes in."

In *Vegas P.I.*, Lake Headley discussed a case that had some cracks. When he tried to see where the light came

in, he almost lost his life. The case involved the murder of an investigative reporter named Don Bolles in Phoenix, Arizona. On June 2, 1976, a car bomb ripped through Bolles's Datsun in a hotel parking lot, mortally wounding him. But Bolles managed to gasp a few words to the people who came to his aid: "They finally got me. The Mafia. Emprise. Find John Adamson."

On the basis of Bolles's final words, Phoenix police began investigating John Harvey Adamson, a local thug. They soon developed evidence that Adamson had lured the reporter to the hotel and planted the car bomb. An attorney named Neal Roberts, a close associate of Adamson, also seemed to have some involvement. In exchange for immunity from prosecution, Roberts implicated a local building contractor, Max Dunlap, and a wealthy rancher and liquor distributor, Kemper Marley. Eight days after the Bolles murder, Dunlap delivered

$5,800 to Adamson at his lawyer's office. Adamson told police this was a payoff from Marley.

Months later, Adamson struck his own deal with prosecutors: he avoided a death sentence by testifying that Dunlap, acting on behalf of Marley, had hired him and James Robison, a plumber he knew, to kill Don Bolles. The motive: a series of articles Bolles had written several years earlier about Marley's supposedly fraudulent business dealings. On the basis of this testimony Dunlap and Robison were convicted of murder and sentenced to die in Arizona's gas chamber. Yet curiously, Marley was never indicted because prosecutors said there was a lack of evidence against him.

Dunlap steadfastly maintained his innocence. He had a simple explanation for the most damning piece of evidence against him, the fact that he had given confessed killer Adamson $5,800. He said that attorney Neal Roberts, a high school classmate of his, had asked him to deliver the money to Adamson's lawyer because he was too busy to do it himself. But the lawyer was out of the office when he arrived, and the receptionist directed him to a room where Adamson, whom Dunlap had never met, was waiting.

The transaction seemed like a setup. And the prosecution's explanation of the murder failed to account for two-thirds of what Don Bolles had uttered before he died: the Mafia and Emprise, a national sports-concession business said to have ties to the mob. In Arizona, Emprise co-owned six dog-racing tracks. Dunlap's friends, refusing to believe he was involved in the murder, started a legal fund and hired a lawyer to represent him on appeal. It was through this lawyer, a friend, that Lake Headley became involved in the case.

The first crack in the prosecution's case came when Headley discovered that Neal Roberts, the lawyer given immunity, had reported two cars and a pickup truck stolen on the day of Don Bolles's murder. One of the vehicles, found on the side of an interstate

The large private detective agencies often provide security for businesses. Here a detective oversees security preparations for a New York fashion show.

highway, had apparently broken down. Another was found at a local airport. The third was never recovered. None of this information had been shared with Dunlap's or Robison's lawyers. Headley believed the vehicles had been used for the real killers' getaways. The idea that three vehicles might be stolen from a key figure in a murder case on the very day of the murder seemed preposterous.

"Often detective work involves the tedious, boring, and mundane, such as reading police reports," Headley explained in *Vegas P.I.* As he pored over police reports from the Bolles case, the private investigator discovered several pieces of crucial information. In one report a Phoenix homicide detective detailed his interview with an acquaintance of Neal Roberts. The acquaintance said that, at a Memorial Day picnic two weeks before the Bolles murder, Roberts and Adamson discussed explosives and getting rid of the reporter. Another report revealed that at the time of his death Bolles had been working on a story involving a scandal at Arizona's dog-racing tracks, and specifically about a racing official named Bradley Funk. Funk happened to be a friend of Neal Roberts. His family also co-owned the six Arizona dog tracks with Emprise.

Headley later located a prisoner who had done time with confessed killer John Adamson after his arrest for the Bolles murder. The prisoner said that Adamson had told him he needed to put together a story before his trial because he didn't want to go to the gas chamber. Adamson's confidante asked why, since he had already been offered immunity in exchange for telling who had ordered the murder, he didn't just tell the truth. He replied that while the state might give immunity, *his* people didn't.

A police informant told Headley that three weeks before the car bombing he had overheard a discussion about killing the reporter. Although he had immediately informed the police, and had later passed the information to the office of Arizona's attorney general, no one ever followed up.

As the investigation gained momentum, a Scottsdale, Arizona, newspaper followed the developments. Finally, a conscience-stricken Phoenix police detective contacted Headley and confessed that he and another detective had been ordered by their superiors to get rid of evidence implicating dog-racing official Bradley Funk. The other detective confirmed the story.

Gaping cracks had appeared in the state's case, and the light that shone through hinted at secrets and corruption at high levels. Funk and Roberts counted among their friends some of Arizona's wealthiest and most prominent citizens, and their business associates apparently included the Mafia. Police had destroyed

evidence; the attorney general's office had ignored a promising line of inquiry. A lot of people seemed interested in seeing the Bolles murder inquiry disposed of with a minimum of digging. Nevertheless, in February 1980 the Arizona Supreme Court overturned the convictions of Max Dunlap and James Robison and ordered new trials.

Headley continued investigating the case, and it nearly cost him his life. On June 21, 1980, an arson fire raced through his apartment as he slept. He spent a week in the hospital in critical condition. Later a firefighter who had been on the scene said Phoenix police detectives had removed files from the apartment. The missing files, according to Headley, concerned his Bolles investigation.

In today's complex business environment, private investigators with advanced degrees in finance or accounting find their services in great demand.

Seattle private investigator and detective agency owner Janet Christensen, who specializes in finding missing persons.

In his new trial, Robison was acquitted of the Bolles murder in 1993. Dunlap, however, was found guilty the following year and sentenced to life in prison. Many investigative journalists continue to believe that the real story has never been told.

In addition to aiding defense lawyers in criminal cases, private investigators play an important role in civil litigation, or lawsuits. Lawyers representing clients in personal-injury lawsuits frequently hire P.I.'s to investigate the facts of the case.

When working for an attorney, whether on a criminal or civil case, a private investigator enjoys the same privileged relationship with the client as does the lawyer. The P.I. cannot be compelled to reveal information about the client, and in fact could not reveal that information even if he or she wanted to. Private investigators who do work for lawyers must be especially vigilant about observing the rules of evidence. Any information gathered through improper or illegal means—for example, by tape-recording a conversation without the second party's consent or by impersonating a police officer—is inadmissible in court, can render any testimony by the P.I. invalid, and can expose him or her to criminal charges.

Private detectives also perform many functions for insurance companies. They may investigate embezzlement, probe suspicious life insurance claims, or find missing heirs. They may check workers' compensation claims, an area that has traditionally been rife with fraud. In the book *Blye, Private Eye*, veteran New York P.I. Irwin Blye describes a simple technique he used to expose people who feigned incapacitating injuries to collect workers' comp. Blye would put heavy weights in these people's garbage cans and then photograph them as they carried the cans to the curb.

Corporate America accounts for a substantial portion of private detective work, especially for large detective agencies. Businesses hire these agencies to provide security, to prevent and investigate the theft of proprietary information, and sometimes to gather information on competitors. Private investigators with degrees in finance or accounting help businesses construct financial profiles of rivals and potential merger partners. And a significant and growing area of corporate detective work involves the investigation of potential employees.

An experienced private detective can produce surprisingly detailed background checks without actually interviewing anyone.

"America," Irwin Blye remarked, "is information-happy and the only trick is in knowing what you want and where to find it."

Public records—including vehicle and voter registration lists, marriage licenses, divorce records, real estate transactions, liens, and court records—have always been legally available to anyone who wants to check them. In the past, however, obtaining them could be time-consuming and frustrating. It was necessary to physically go to a county courthouse and search the records, and unless certain information about the person being investigated was already known, there was no guarantee that the records sought would be at a given courthouse. Advances in computer technology have changed that. Database searches can quickly turn up a person's public records—and, if the individual doing the searching knows his or her way around cyberspace, a considerable amount of supposedly private information as well. And market research firms now collect—and sell—demographic, consumption, and lifestyle data on most American consumers. Taken individually, the pieces of information that make up a consumer profile—collected from such routine sources as magazine subscriptions, airline ticket purchases, and product warranties—aren't particularly revealing. Together, however, these discrete bits of information can shed light on a person's interests, income, spending patterns, and private life.

Of course, the government maintains massive databases as well. The Internal Revenue Service (IRS) has records on everyone who has filed a tax return. The FBI's National Crime Information Center (NCIC), which went on-line in 1967, contains files not only on virtually everyone charged with a crime but also on "suspicious persons" and on victims, witnesses, and close relatives and associates of anyone who was the subject of an FBI investigation. Anyone who has ever received a speeding ticket, complained of a mistake in a government check, or written to the president at the White House should also have a file on the FBI database. The computer that contains the database, housed in the temperature-controlled basement of FBI headquarters and maintained and operated 24 hours a day by a team of technicians, is the size of a football field. By

The J. Edgar Hoover F.B.I. Building houses the massive NCIC database. Although the database is supposed to be off-limits to everyone except official law enforcement agents, private investigators have found ways to skirt the rules.

matching its records with ones available every day from the private sector—airline ticket purchases, hotel registrations, ATM transactions—the FBI can theoretically monitor the movements of anyone it has a file on. And that constitutes 8 percent or more of the population of the United States.

Today the NCIC computer is accessed about 2.5 million times each day through 97,000 terminals serving about 70,000 police and other federal agencies. According to author Diarmuid Jeffreys, the system has approximately 500,000 authorized users.

In theory, FBI and other government databases are off-limits to private investigators. But according to some sources, circumventing the rules isn't particularly difficult. Many private investigators are themselves former police officers, and they maintain contacts with their old colleagues. And those who can't gain access through contacts in law enforcement can turn to information brokers, unauthorized users willing to access a database for a fee. One such broker, a private detective named Allen Schweitzer, emphasized the ease with which a P.I. could get information from the FBI's NCIC database:

> The NCIC computer system is supposedly policed by the FBI. They are supposed to maintain its integrity. But they are not doing their job. I mean, almost every private eye in the country has access to this in one way, shape, or form, either through a broker like me, or because they have their own law enforcement sources.

In the early 1980s, Schweitzer, an apprentice private detective for a firm in California's Silicon Valley, came to two realizations: first, he didn't much care for the tedious, time-honored methods of surveillance and information gathering; and second, other P.I.'s with similar views would be willing to pay someone to pull confidential information from computer databases they could not legally access. Schweitzer developed a network of sources who had access to large databases—people who worked for the phone company, credit bureaus, banks, local government agencies, and, most important of all, law enforcement agencies. Soon business was booming. Customers were given a brochure that listed by code number the databases to which he had access:

> If a client wanted NCIC or criminal history information, they would give me the name and date of birth, and sometimes the Social Security number, which is helpful if you have a John Smith or whatever. At the end of the day, typically, I'd have one request, two requests, maybe ten requests for NCIC information, and I would call one

of my sources within the law enforcement community, whether it be in the state police, the local police, or in a federal law enforcement agency. I'd give him the subject's information and I would get it back from him the next morning via the fax.

His clients even included law enforcement agents who needed information that they couldn't legally get or who didn't want to wait days to get a subpoena for information Schweitzer could provide in minutes (unlisted telephone numbers, records of toll calls, and the like).

In 1988 Schweitzer was caught trying to enter an IRS database. He was released on the condition that he cooperate with the FBI and IRS in uncovering other information brokers and that he give up his illegal activities. But he was soon back in business. After another arrest, he was sentenced to four years' probation and community service. On July 6, 1992, Schweitzer received a request to testify before the House Subcommittee on Civil and Constitutional Rights about the sale of criminal-history records. But the request was soon withdrawn because "it was causing the committee too many embarrassing problems with the Department of Justice."

The case of Allen Schweitzer illustrates the potential for abuse inherent in arrangements that bring private or quasi-official agents into the public realm of law enforcement. Of course, private investigators and bounty hunters have no monopoly on law enforcement abuses, but they function under far less scrutiny and oversight than do the police.

In spite of this, P.I.'s and bounty hunters continue to play an indispensable role in supplementing official law enforcement, as they have for more than 150 years. Whether or not greater regulation of the two professions is imposed, they will probably always occupy a vital niche in the American justice system.

Further Reading

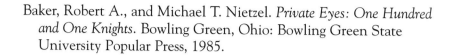

Baker, Robert A., and Michael T. Nietzel. *Private Eyes: One Hundred and One Knights*. Bowling Green, Ohio: Bowling Green State University Popular Press, 1985.

Drimmer, Jonathan. "When Man Hunts Man: The Rights and Duties of Bounty Hunters in the American Criminal Justice System." *Houston Law Review* 33, 3 (Fall 1996): 731-793.

Goulart, Ron. *The Dime Detectives*. New York: The Mysterious Press, 1988.

Headley, Lake, with William Hoffman. *Vegas P.I.* New York: Thunder's Mouth Press, 1993.

Jeffreys, Diarmuid. *The Bureau: Inside the Modern FBI*. Boston: Houghton Mifflin, 1995.

Krakel, Dean F. *The Saga of Tom Horn: The Story of a Cattleman's War*. Lincoln: University of Nebraska Press, 1988.

Morn, Frank. *The Eye That Never Sleeps*. Bloomington: Indiana University Press, 1982.

Pileggi, Nicholas. *Blye, Private Eye*. Chicago: Playboy Books, 1987 (paperback).

Sedgwick, John. *Night Vision: Confessions of Gil Lewis, Private Eye*. New York: Simon & Schuster, 1982.

Index

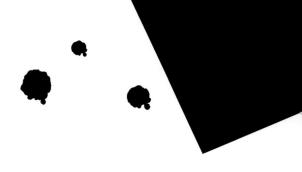

Picture Credits

ANN G. GAINES, a freelance writer who lives in Gonzales, Texas, is the author of many books for young adults. She has master's degrees in Library Science and American Civilization from the University of Texas at Austin.

AUSTIN SARAT is William Nelson Cromwell Professor of Jurisprudence and Political Science at Amherst College, where he also chairs the Department of Law, Jurisprudence and Social Thought. Professor Sarat is the author or editor of 23 books and numerous scholarly articles. Among his books are *Law's Violence*, *Sitting in Judgment: Sentencing the White Collar Criminal*, and *Justice and Injustice in Law and Legal Theory*. He has received many academic awards and held several prestigious fellowships. He is President of the Law & Society Association and Chair of the Working Group on Law, Culture and the Humanities. In addition, he is a nationally recognized teacher and educator whose teaching has been featured in the *New York Times*, on the *Today* show, and on National Public Radio's *Fresh Air*.